LIVING EXPENSES KNOW-HOW

Reading Strategies by Objective

CAMBRIDGE Adult Education
Prentice Hall Regents, Englewood Cliffs, NJ 07632

Writer and Reading Consultant: *Marilyn Meltzer,* Hunter College,
City University of New York

Project Editor: *Jerry Long*
Contributing Editors: *Mike Topp and Elliott Vanskike*
Interior Design: *Lorraine Mullaney*
Cover Design: *Edgar Blakeney*

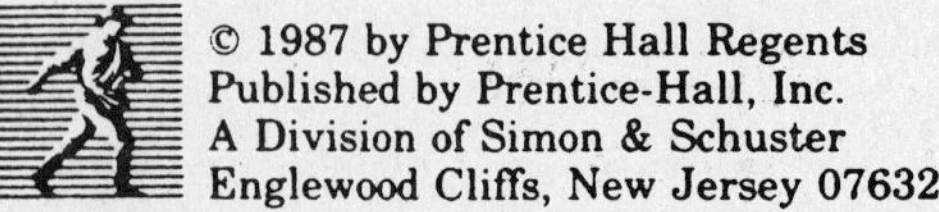

© 1987 by Prentice Hall Regents
Published by Prentice-Hall, Inc.
A Division of Simon & Schuster
Englewood Cliffs, New Jersey 07632

Printed in the United States of America

10 9 8 7 6 5 4 3 2 1

ISBN 0-8428-7406-2

Prentice-Hall International (UK) Limited, *London*
Prentice-Hall of Australia Pty. Limited, *Sydney*
Prentice-Hall Canada Inc., *Toronto*
Prentice-Hall Hispanoamericana, S.A., *Mexico*
Prentice-Hall of India Private Limited, *New Delhi*
Prentice-Hall of Japan, Inc., *Tokyo*
Simon & Schuster Asia Pte. Ltd., *Singapore*
Editora Prentice-Hall do Brasil, Ltda., *Rio de Janeiro*

CONTENTS

TO THE USER

LIFE SKILLS BY OBJECTIVES

The Know-How series contains practical readings on looking for work, holding a job, worker rights, banking, taxes, insurance and consumer advice. These various topics, culled from the Consumer Affairs and Employment areas of the Adult Performance Level study, first appear in each lesson as five learning objectives. The activities and instruction that follow are then keyed to these five objectives.

READING SKILLS BY OBJECTIVES

The Know-How series is also a **reading program**. Using the best of **"mastery learning"** techniques, the Know-How books teach basic reading skills such as finding the main idea, drawing inferences, recalling detail and building vocabulary.

FREQUENT CHECKS FOR MASTERY

Each lesson in the Know-How books follows a consistent format:

Pre-Check—five pre-reading questions designed to focus the reader's attention on the topics to follow, one question for each objective.

Reading passage—easy-reading selections of approximately 250 words that match the objectives one for one.

Review of Key Words—a completion exercise that reinforces the vocabulary from the lesson.

Check What You Know—five multiple choice questions and five fill-in-the-blank questions on the reading. The questions test mastery of each objective.

Number of Right Answers—an activity for calculating level of mastery and for determining if follow-up is needed.

Double Check—a review exercise for those students who need further study.

PRE-TEST AND POST-TEST

The Know-How books begin with a twenty-question multiple choice test which can detect the life competencies and reading skills most in need of attention and can also indicate the lessons appropriate to meet the need. A Post-Test of the same design allows for a final check for mastery and a guide to re-teaching.

SELF-EVALUATION

The answer section provides more than merely the answers to each test and exercise in the book. Each answer is accompanied by the objective the question measures, the skill the question targets, and the competency the question checks. The lesson from which each question was drawn is also given to make review easier.

Pre-Test

DIRECTIONS: Circle the letter of the best answer.

1. Where you live
   a. is something you cannot control.
   b. affects your life in many ways.
   c. is not important.
   d. never changes.

2. Real estate taxes are paid by
   a. the broker.
   b. the renter.
   c. the owner.
   d. the bank.

3. A lease protects
   a. only the renter.
   b. both the owner and the renter.
   c. only the owner.
   d. no one.

4. A mortgage is
   a. a lease.
   b. a down payment.
   c. a gift.
   d. a loan.

5. You can find a place to live from
   a. landlords.
   b. realtors.
   c. signs.
   d. all of the above.

6. The abbreviation lg means
   a. large.
   b. living room.
   c. dining room.
   d. furnished.

7.   A realtor helps people find housing
   a.   to give a free service.
   b.   for pay.
   c.   to save time.
   d.   to help the owner.

8.   Someone is called a landlord because he or she owns
   a.   real estate.
   b.   clothing.
   c.   jewels.
   d.   records.

9.   Smart shoppers
   a.   have a system.
   b.   are lucky.
   c.   spend too much money.
   d.   never spend money.

10.   Often you save money
   a.   buying the smaller size of a product.
   b.   buying the larger size of a product.
   c.   buying a well-known brand.
   d.   buying frozen foods.

11.   To be a good shopper
   a.   you should read the labels.
   b.   tear off all labels.
   c.   ignore all labels.
   d.   replace any missing labels.

12.   The price per ounce, quart, pound, or count is
   a.   the net weight.
   b.   the house brand.
   c.   the unit price.
   d.   the "no frills" brand.

13.   When you shop you should
   a.   buy what you want.
   b.   buy each special.
   c.   only buy items using coupons.
   d.   keep track of what you spend.

14. The highest grade of meat is
    a. good.
    b. prime.
    c. choice.
    d. fair.

15. You should eat from the four basic food groups to
    a. have a balanced diet.
    b. spend less on food.
    c. avoid eating meat.
    d. eat only fruit.

16. Coupons help you
    a. save money on your food bill.
    b. add money to your food bill.
    c. organize your shopping.
    d. keep busy.

17. It often pays to repair your car if
    a. it has been driven less than 50,000 miles.
    b. your warranty has not expired.
    c. you can do it yourself.
    d. all of the above.

18. You pay most for a used car if you buy it from
    a. new car dealers.
    b. used car dealers.
    c. private owners.
    d. your friends.

19. New car dealers will
    a. sell you only new cars.
    b. sell at the lowest prices.
    c. charge you higher prices.
    d. sell only used cars.

20. The *Blue Book*
    a. lists expensive cars.
    b. lists price ranges all over the United States.
    c. lists blue cars.
    d. lists only used cars.

Check your answers on page 51.

LESSON
1

How to Decide About Housing

WHAT YOU WILL LEARN

OBJECTIVE 1   Things to think about when deciding on a new home.

OBJECTIVE 2   Deciding whether you can afford to rent or buy.

OBJECTIVE 3   Deciding whether you should rent or buy.

OBJECTIVE 4   Figuring how much space you need.

OBJECTIVE 5   Choosing where you want to live.

PRE-CHECK

DIRECTIONS: Check your *purpose* for reading. Each statement that follows is about one objective of the lesson. Read the statement. Then, put a check under your reason for reading each objective.

		YES, BUT I WANT TO REVIEW	NO, I WILL READ TO LEARN
1.	Can you list three things to think about when you want a new home?	_______	_______
2.	Do you know the percent of income you would spend on housing?	_______	_______
3.	Can you list three things good about renting and three things good about owning a house?	_______	_______
4.	Can you list three questions to figure how much living space you need?	_______	_______
5.	Can you list three things to keep in mind when you are choosing a place to live?	_______	_______

4

PREVIEW

DIRECTIONS: Before you read the whole lesson:

1. Read the title of the lesson.
2. Read the key words and their definitions.
3. Read the titles of each objective in the lesson.
4. Read the first sentence under each objective.

Now, you have previewed the reading. See if you can check the right answer for the following sentence.

You need a new place to live. You don't need to think about

☐   a. how much money you can afford to spend.

☐   b. how much space you'll need.

☐   c. how much your new car costs.

Did you check *c*? Then you are ready to begin reading.

Key Words

1. **down payment**   part of the total cost that has to be paid right away, before you can take out a loan for the rest of the cost.

2. **equity**   the money value of a property. As you make mortgage payments on a house, you build up your equity.

3. **lease**   a written contract for rental. The lease states the rent, the rental time, and the rights of the owner and renter.

4. **mortgage**   the loan you get from the bank when you buy housing.

5. **rental deposit**   money paid to the owner when the lease is signed. It is to cover damage caused by the renter. The deposit is returned at the end of the lease period, if no damage was caused.

1 THINGS TO THINK ABOUT WHEN DECIDING ON A NEW HOME

You may not have to decide on housing very often. But when you do, you have to "live" with your decision. Where you live affects your life in many ways.

There are several things to think about when you need a new home.

- The amount of money you can afford to spend on housing
- The amount of space you need
- Whether you want to rent or buy
- Where you want to live

2 DECIDING WHETHER YOU CAN AFFORD TO RENT OR BUY

How Much Rent Can You Afford to Pay?

Your housing costs include expenses in addition to rent. Housing costs also include payments for water, gas, oil, electric, and phone service.

Many people figure that one-fourth, or 25%, of the family income after taxes is what they should spend on housing. Each month, one week's income would be spent on housing.

However, a realistic figure today might be 30%, or almost one-third, of income. This amount is needed in cities, where housing costs can be high.

Can you Afford to Buy a House?

Many people have their hearts set on owning their own home. But if you want to buy a house, remember, the cost of your house should not be more than $2\frac{1}{2}$ times your total yearly income before taxes. So, for example, if you earned $10,000 a year before taxes, you would be able to afford a house costing $25,000.

Can You Afford the Down Payment?

When you buy a home you pay part of the total cost of the house right away. This is known as the down payment. A down payment may be as little as 10% of the total price of a house. It could be higher, too—as much as 25% or 30%, or even more.

For example, you want to buy a house on sale for $66,000. Your down payment is 25% of the price in cash.

$$25\% = \tfrac{1}{4}$$
$$\tfrac{1}{4} \times \$66,000 = \$66,000 \div 4 = \$16,500.$$

So you must have $16,500 in cash for your down payment.

Can You Afford the Mortgage?

After you pay the down payment, you must borrow money to pay the rest of the price. A bank (or another lender) will lend you the money. The money is paid to the seller. Then you must repay the loan, or **mortgage,** over a certain number of years.

Of course, the bank will charge you interest on the money you borrowed. This is an extra amount of money returned with the amount you borrowed. Interest is charged as a percent of the amount you borrowed. This percent is called the interest rate. Interest rates change from time to time. They change from one part of the country to another, and even from bank to bank. Shop around for the lowest interest rate when you want to get a mortgage.

OBJECTIVE

3   DECIDING WHETHER YOU SHOULD RENT OR BUY

There are several good points to renting.

Things to Think About in Renting

- **No upkeep**   the owner pays all major repairs and maintains the home.
- **No real estate taxes**   the owner pays the taxes.

- **Less cash up front**   you put down a rental deposit along with the first month's rent. This money is paid to the owner when you sign the lease. It is security money, to be used for repairs if you cause any damage to the property. If you cause no damage, the money is returned to you when you move.
- **Easier to move**   if you have no lease, or written contract for rental, you can move out at the end of any month. If you do have a lease, you can move out when the lease is up.

Things to Think About in Buying

There are several points, both good and bad, to owning a home.

- **Equity**   with each mortgage payment you make, you own a larger share of your house. This is your equity, your share of the total value of your house. Owning property is an investment, because you are building up equity every month.
- **Taxes**   as an owner, you have to pay real estate taxes. These taxes can be taken off, or deducted from, your income tax payments. The interest on your mortgage can also be deducted from your income taxes.
- **Collateral and credit**   as you build up equity, you can use your share of ownership as collateral for another loan.

OBJECTIVE

4 FIGURING HOW MUCH SPACE YOU NEED

The larger a house or an apartment, the more it costs. First, decide how much you can spend on housing. Then, decide how large an apartment or house you can afford. Here are some things to think about when you decide about space needs:

- How many bedrooms do you and your family need?
- Do you and your family need outdoor space?
- Can you divide the rooms into separate areas?

OBJECTIVE

5 CHOOSING WHERE YOU WANT TO LIVE

Where you live depends on your family's needs. Here are some things to think about when you are deciding where to move.

- Do you need public transportation to get to work?
- Are you near a road or highway?
- Do you want to live near your relatives?
- Do you want to be close to the shopping areas?
- Do you want to be able to walk to a house of worship?
- Do you want to live near a school or a park?

Make a list of your needs. Then decide where you want to live.

REVIEW OF KEY WORDS

DIRECTIONS: Fill in each blank in the paragraph with a term from the list that follows.

mortgage   **equity**   **rental deposit**
lease   **down payment**

Cynthia wanted to move out of her apartment. She could move because the _______________ was up. She
(1)
had not damaged the apartment, so her _______________
(2)
was returned. She decided to buy a house. Month after month, she would be building _______________ which
(3)
is a good investment. She had money saved to pay the _______________ right away. Then Cynthia went to a
(4)
bank. She asked for a _______________ to pay for the
(5)
rest of the cost.

Check your answers on page 52.

CHECK WHAT YOU KNOW

DIRECTIONS: Circle the letter of the best answer.

1. Money, space, and the area you will live in are some things to think about when you are
   a. deciding about housing.
   b. choosing a school.
   c. selecting a house of worship.
   d. buying a new car.

2. To decide how much you can afford to pay in rent, you should figure
   a. one-fifth of monthly income before taxes.
   b. one-fourth to one-third of monthly take-home pay.
   c. one-third to one-half of monthly income before taxes.
   d. one-fifth of monthly take-home pay.

3. One advantage of renting rather than buying a home is
   a. you cannot make any changes in the home without asking the owner.
   b. you have to give a rental deposit to the owner before you move in.
   c. you have to sign a lease with the owner.
   d. the owner takes care of all major repairs.

4. In thinking about how much space you need in housing, you should
   a. select the largest place that you can find.
   b. ask your family how much space they need.
   c. first figure out how much you can afford to pay.
   d. always live in a house with one extra room.

5. When looking for a neighborhood, it's best to
   a. think about nearness to public transportation, schools, and shopping centers.
   b. visit each town within two miles of the place where you work.
   c. choose a place where your friends live.
   d. be sure that you can walk to work.

DIRECTIONS: Fill in each blank with the correct words.

6. Where you live affects your ________________ in many ways.

7. A house should not cost more than ________________ times your yearly net income.

8. As an owner you have to pay ________________ taxes.

9. The larger a house is, the ________________ it will cost.

10. Where you live depends on your family's __________.

Check your answers on page 52.

Number of Right Answers

REVIEW OF KEY WORDS __________

CHECK WHAT YOU KNOW __________

If you got seven or more answers right on "Check What You Know," you are ready to go on to "Using What You Know." If you got fewer than seven answers right, review this lesson. Re-read the objective for each question you missed. Then try to answer the "Double Check" questions that follow.

DOUBLE CHECK

DIRECTIONS: Match the term in **Column A** with its definition in **Column B.** Write the correct letter beside each number.

COLUMN A	COLUMN B
____ 1. Mortgage	a. the money value of property
____ 2. Lease	b. loan
____ 3. Equity	c. something to think about when you decide where to live
____ 4. Distance to shopping areas	d. written contract for rental
____ 5. Number of bedrooms	e. a space need

Check your answers on page 52.

USING WHAT YOU KNOW

Josephine got a new job and needed to move to a different state. Listed below are some of the things she had to think about before she decided if she wanted to rent an apartment or own a house. Put a check in the RENT column for those items that apply to renting an apartment. Put a check in the OWN column for those items that apply to owning a house.

	RENT	OWN
1. Builds equity	☐	☐
2. Down payment needed	☐	☐
3. You can move out at the end of any month	☐	☐
4. Less cash needed right away	☐	☐
5. No real estate taxes	☐	☐
6. You can use as collateral	☐	☐
7. Is an investment	☐	☐
8. You pay for repairs and upkeep	☐	☐
9. You deduct interest from income tax	☐	☐
10. You develop credit rating	☐	☐

Check your answers on page 52.

LESSON 2

Finding a Place to Live

WHAT YOU WILL LEARN

OBJECTIVE 1 How to find a place to live.

OBJECTIVE 2 Understanding different kinds of housing.

OBJECTIVE 3 How to read newspaper ads to find housing.

OBJECTIVE 4 How to work with a real estate agent.

OBJECTIVE 5 People you deal with after you sign the lease.

PRE-CHECK

DIRECTIONS: Check your *purpose* for reading. Each statement that follows is about one objective of the lesson. Read the statement. Then, put a check under your reason for reading that objective.

		YES, BUT I WANT TO REVIEW	NO, I WILL READ TO LEARN
1.	Can you list three ways to find a place to live?	________	________
2.	Can you list two kinds of housing?	________	________
3.	Do you know what the abbreviations in newspaper ads mean?	________	________
4.	Can you explain how a real estate agent or broker can help you find a place to live?	________	________
5.	Do you know which people you deal with after you sign a lease?	________	________

PREVIEW

DIRECTIONS: Before you read the whole lesson:

1.   Read the title of the lesson.
2.   Read the key words and their definitions.
3.   Read the titles of each objective in the lesson.
4.   Read the first sentence of each objective.

Now, you have previewed the reading. See if you can check the correct answer for the following sentence.

When you are trying to find a place to live, you should

☐   a. make a quick choice.

☐   b. lose your patience.

☐   c. look at newspaper ads.

If you checked *c*, then you are ready to begin.

Key Words

1.   **efficiency apartment**   a one-room apartment. It does not have a separate kitchen.
2.   **landlord**   a person who owns apartment buildings. You rent an apartment from a landlord.
3.   **realtor**   a person who sells or rents housing. A realtor is also called a real estate agent, or a broker.
4.   **studio apartment**   a one-room apartment that has a separate kitchen. A studio is sometimes called a $1\frac{1}{2}$ room apartment.
5.   **tenant**   a person who rents or leases an apartment or house. A tenant pays rent to the landlord.

OBJECTIVE

1 HOW TO FIND A PLACE TO LIVE

You have thought about cost, space, and where you want to live. Once you have taken these first steps to finding housing, you are ready to search for a place to live. You may be in a hurry to move. But you may have problems if you make a quick choice.

There are many different ways to find housing. You might walk through the streets looking for "For Rent" or "For Sale" signs. Ask friends if they know of any available housing. Sometimes you can find the best housing through newspaper ads and **realtors.**

Realtors sell or rent houses and apartments. Realtors and *landlords*, or owners, place housing ads in the paper. When you answer an ad, you will be talking to the realtor or landlord.

2 UNDERSTANDING DIFFERENT KINDS OF HOUSING

You can either rent or buy a house or an apartment. There are several types of apartments that are available:

- **efficiency apartment** one-room apartment. An efficiency apartment does not have a separate kitchen.
- **studio apartment** a one-room apartment that has a separate kitchen. A studio is sometimes called a $1\frac{1}{2}$ room apartment.
- **apartment** an apartment that has one or more bedrooms.
- **duplex** an apartment that has rooms on two floors.

3 HOW TO READ NEWSPAPER ADS TO FIND HOUSING

When you read housing ads in the newspaper, you have to know what the abbreviations mean. The abbreviations used in many newspaper ads are listed below:

app appliances
BR bedroom
Inq Supt inquire of superintendent
Eves/wknds evenings and weekends
G & E incl gas and electric included

furn furnished
bth bathroom
per mo per month
conv transp convenient to transportation
D/W dishwasher
lg large
reqd required
util utilities
w to w crpt wall-to-wall carpeting
apt apartment
LR living room
A/C air conditioning
mod modern
rms rooms
sep kit separate kitchen
unf unfurnished
DR dining room
nr near
drps drapes

OBJECTIVE

4 HOW TO WORK WITH A REALTOR

Realtors are also called real estate agents, or real estate brokers. They rent or sell housing for the landlord. Realtors charge for their services. Often the owner pays the fee. The person buying or renting may also be asked to pay the fee. Realtors know what housing is available. This can save you a lot of time when you are looking for a place to live.

OBJECTIVE

5 PEOPLE YOU DEAL WITH AFTER YOU SIGN THE LEASE

You may rent through a realtor, but the realtor's job is done when you sign the lease. After that, you are a **tenant,** or renter. Once you have rented the housing, you deal with the landlord. Your landlord might have hired a manager to take care of the building. Then you would deal with the manager.

REVIEW OF KEY WORDS

DIRECTIONS: Fill in each blank in the paragraph with a term from the list that follows:

**landlord   studio apartment   realtor
tenant   efficiency apartment**

John wanted to rent an apartment. He asked a ______________ to help him find an _______________, which did
(1)   (2)
not have a separate kitchen. He preferred a ______________,
(3)
which had a separate kitchen. The broker said that the owner, or ______________, would pay his fee. John was a
(4)
______________. He was just renting the apartment. He had
(5)
to pay the owner a month's rent.

Check your answers on page 53.

CHECK WHAT YOU KNOW

DIRECTIONS: Circle the letter of the best answer.

1. You've made some decisions about costs, space, and where you want to live. You're ready to
   a. sign a lease.
   b. learn how to travel to work by car.
   c. find a place to live.
   d. fix up your present home.

2. An apartment without a separate kitchen is called
   a. a studio.
   b. an efficiency apartment.
   c. a duplex.
   d. a two-bedroom apartment.

3. The abbreviation *w to w crpt* means
   a. wall-to-wall carpeting.
   b. utilities.
   c. appliances.
   d. rooms.

4. Sometimes people don't use realtors to help them find housing because
    a. they want to save the realtor's fee, or charge.
    b. brokers only show costly housing.
    c. they don't know any brokers.
    d. the ads in the paper are the best rentals.

5. A tenant is someone who
    a. rents.
    b. buys.
    c. sells.
    d. manages.

DIRECTIONS: Fill in each blank with the correct words.

6. Ask friends if they know of any ______________ housing.

7. A ______________ apartment has rooms of two floors.

8. *Eves/wknds* means ______________.

9. Often the owner pays a broker's ______________.

10. Your landlord might hire someone to ______________ the building.

Check your answers on page 53.

Number of Right Answers

REVIEW OF KEY WORDS ______________

CHECK WHAT YOU KNOW ______________

If you got seven or more correct answers on "Check What You Know," you are ready to go on to "Using What You Know." If you got fewer than seven answers right, review this lesson. Re-read the objective for each question you missed. Then try to answer the "Double Check" questions that follow.

DOUBLE CHECK

DIRECTIONS: Match the term in **Column A** with its definition in **Column B.** Write the correct letter beside each number.

COLUMN A	COLUMN B
____ 1. Realtor	a. owner
____ 2. Landlord	b. $1\frac{1}{2}$ room apartment
____ 3. Mod	c. renter
____ 4. Studio	d. modern
____ 5. Tenant	e. real estate agent

Check your answers on page 53.

USING WHAT YOU KNOW

On page 14, there is a list of abbreviations and terms usually found in newspaper ads. Read this list, and then read the newspaper ad below. Put a check beside each question you would need to ask.

One BR apt on Jefferson. Stove and refrigerator, furn. Deposit and references. reqd. Lease. Call 453-3563.

1. _________ How much is the rent?

2. _________ How many bedrooms?

3. _________ Are utilities included?

4. _________ What is the address?

5. _________ How much is the deposit?

6. _________ How long is the lease?

7. _________ Is it furnished?

8. _________ Are appliances included?

9. _________ Walk-up or elevator?

10. _________ What street is it on?

Check your answers on page 53.

LESSON
3

How You Can Become
a Better Shopper

WHAT YOU WILL LEARN

OBJECTIVE 1   How to learn food shopping skills.

OBJECTIVE 2   How to comparison shop.

OBJECTIVE 3   How to use unit prices to compare costs.

OBJECTIVE 4   How to compare quality, taste, and nutrition.

OBJECTIVE 5   How to read labels.

PRE-CHECK

DIRECTIONS: Check your *purpose* for reading. Each statement that follows is about one objective of the lesson. Read each statement. Then put a check under your reason for reading that objective.

		YES, BUT I WANT TO REVIEW	NO, I WILL READ TO LEARN
1.	Can you list three food shopping skills?	________	________
2.	Do you know how to comparison shop?	________	________
3.	Can you figure unit prices?	________	________
4.	Can you list two other kinds of products besides nationally advertised brands?	________	________
5.	Do you read labels when you shop?	________	________

PREVIEW

DIRECTIONS: Before you read the whole lesson:

1. Read the title of the lesson.
2. Read the key words and their definitions.
3. Read the titles of each objective in the lesson.
4. Read the first sentence of each objective.

Now you have previewed the reading. See if you can check the right answer for the following sentence.

When you shop for food, you should

☐   a. read labels.

☐   b. spend a lot of money.

☐   c. drive to the nearest store.

Did you check *a*? Then you are ready to begin.

Key Words

1. **generic products**   products that come in plain packages. They are lower in price than nationally advertised brands. They are often lower in quality.
2. **house brands**   items that carry the store's label. They are often as good as nationally advertised brands, but they cost less.
3. **net weight**   the weight of a product itself. The weight of the package is not included.
4. **Recommended Daily Allowance (RDA)**   the amount of protein, vitamins, and other nutrients in a product.
5. **unit price**   the price per ounce, pound, or count.

OBJECTIVE
1 FOOD SHOPPING SKILLS

Food shopping is a skill that each person needs to learn. You want to eat well, but you also want to have some money left after leaving the check-out line. Smart shoppers develop a system for doing this. They learn as much as they can about food and nutrition. They read the ads from their local stores. They plan each shopping trip carefully. They get the most for their money by reading labels and knowing how to compare the prices of different items.

OBJECTIVE
2 HOW TO COMPARISON SHOP

Comparison shopping means many things:

- Comparing costs of different brands of the same food item
- Measuring costs and nutritional value of different food items
- Contrasting values, sales, and shopping in different stores

OBJECTIVE
3 HOW TO USE UNIT PRICES TO COMPARE COSTS

The **unit price** of an item is the price per ounce, quart, pound, or count. Knowing the unit price of an item helps you compare the costs of buying different-sized packages of the same brand. It also helps you compare the costs of different brands. In most places, stores are required by law to place unit price labels on the package or on the store's shelves. Sometimes, you can save money by buying the larger size of the same product.

4 HOW TO COMPARE QUALITY, TASTE, AND NUTRITION

Quality can be just as important as unit price. For example, one dishwashing liquid may cost less per ounce than another brand. But, you may need to use more of it to get the same effect. Then it is not a bargain. Good shoppers learn through trial and error. They know what to expect from a certain food or product.

Many stores carry their own "house brand" of products. A **house brand** usually costs less than a nationally advertised brand. House brands are sometimes made by the same producers that make the more costly brands. Since the house brand is not advertised, it is often cheaper.

You may also see "no frills" or **generic** products in your store. Generic products often come in very simple packages. They are cheaper than the nationally advertised brands and the house brands. They are usually lower in quality. But the products are still nutritious.

5 HOW TO READ LABELS

All manufactured food products must be labeled. The label on the package must tell:

- The name and address of the company that made, packaged, or shipped the product
- The **net weight** of the contents—the weight of the product itself
- The ingredients in the product
- Other facts, such as nutrition information, the size of an average serving, and the number of servings per package.

By comparing labels you can tell which foods are the best sources of certain vitamins and nutrients. Reading labels can help you figure out how much nutrition you are getting for your money.

The label gives you information about the **Recommended Daily Allowance** (RDA). The RDA is the amount of a vitamin or mineral a person needs each day to stay healthy.

REVIEW OF KEY WORDS

DIRECTIONS: Fill in each blank in the paragraph with a term from the list that follows.

RDA   **house brand**   **unit price**
generic product   **net weight**

Rose went to the store. She looked at the price per quart of milk so she could figure out the _______________.
(1)
She wanted to buy a product as good as a nationally advertised brand, so she bought a _______________. If
(2)
she didn't care if the quality was lower, she would have bought a _______________. She wanted to know the
(3)
_______________, the weight of the product itself. She
(4)
also wanted to find out the Recommended Daily Allowance of nutrients, so she read the _______________.
(5)

Check your answers on page 54.

CHECK WHAT YOU KNOW

DIRECTIONS: Circle the letter of the best answer.

1.   To be a better shopper, you have to learn how to
      a.   cook.
      b.   comparison shop.
      c.   shop every day.
      d.   shop with a friend.

2. When you shop, you should compare all but the
    a. cost.
    b. size of the store.
    c. nutritional value.
    d. convenience.

3. If ten oranges cost $1.50, the unit price is
    a. $ .15.
    b. $ 1.50.
    c. $15.00.
    d. $ .30.

4. "Trial and error" shopping means
    a. always making mistakes.
    b. never trying new things.
    c. trying new things, making mistakes, and then
        learning from your mistakes.
    d. never making mistakes.

5. Facts on labels tell you everything but the
    a. address of the company that packaged the prod-
        uct.
    b. amount of protein in the product.
    c. RDA.
    d. taste.

DIRECTIONS: Fill in each blank with the correct words.

6. _________________ is a skill each person needs to
learn.

7. _________________ shopping means many things.

8. Knowing the _______________ price of an item
can help you save money.

9. _______________ can be just as important as the
unit price.

10. All manufactured food products must be _________.

Check your answers on page 54.

Number of Right Answers

REVIEW OF KEY WORDS   ________

CHECK WHAT YOU KNOW   ________

If you got seven or more correct answers on "Check What You Know," you are ready to go on to "Using What You Know." If you got fewer than seven answers right, review this lesson. Re-read the objective for each question you missed. Then try to answer the "Double Check" questions that follow.

DOUBLE CHECK

DIRECTIONS: Match the term in **Column A** with its definition in **Column B.** Write the correct letter beside each number.

COLUMN A	COLUMN B
____ 1. Food shopping skill	a. price per ounce, quart, pound, or count
____ 2. Comparison shopping	b. "no frills" brand
____ 3. Generic product	c. reading ads from local stores
____ 4. Unit price	d. contrasting sales in store
____ 5. Net weight	e. weight of the product

Check your answers on page 54.

USING WHAT YOU KNOW

Look at the list of items below. Figure out the unit price. Then put a check next to the item that is the best buy.

☐   1.   6 ounces of detergent for $ .99

☐   2. 12 ounces of detergent for $1.50

☐   3. 18 ounces of detergent for $2.25

☐   4. 24 ounces of detergent for $2.80

☐   5. 30 ounces of detergent for $3.75

Check your answers on page 54.

Food Shopping

WHAT YOU WILL LEARN

OBJECTIVE 1   Making your shopping list.

OBJECTIVE 2   Smart shopping.

OBJECTIVE 3   Buying good food.

OBJECTIVE 4   Understanding the grades of meat.

OBJECTIVE 5   The four basic food groups.

PRE-CHECK

DIRECTIONS: Decide on your *purpose* for reading. Each statement that follows is about one objective of the lesson. Read the statement. Then, put a check under your reason for reading that objective.

		YES, BUT I WANT TO REVIEW	NO, I WILL READ TO LEARN
1.	Can you name four steps in making a shopping list?		
2.	Can you list two ways to save money when you go shopping?		
3.	Do you know why you should read labels on packages?		
4.	Can you list the three grades of meat?		
5.	Can you name the four basic food groups?		

PREVIEW

DIRECTIONS: Before you read the whole lesson:

1.   Read the title of the lesson.
2.   Read the key words and their definitions.
3.   Read the title of each objective in the lesson.
4.   Read the first sentence under each objective.

Now, you have previewed the reading. See if you can check the correct answer for the following sentence.

To follow your food budget, you should not

☐   a. check ads before you go shopping.

☐   b. shop when you are hungry.

☐   c. ask for specials.

Did you check *b*? Then you are ready to begin reading.

Key Words

1.   **groceries**   food and household supplies.
2.   **coupon**   part of a printed ad to be cut out and given to the person at the check-out counter. A coupon tells how much money you can save on your food bill.
3.   **grade**   type or kind. How good something is.
4.   **perishable food**   products that are likely to spoil. Be careful how you store perishable foods.
5.   **specials**   good buys, sales. You should try to watch for specials when you shop.

OBJECTIVE

1   MAKING YOUR SHOPPING LIST

The most important thing to do before you go shopping for **groceries** is to make a list of what you need. Look in your refrigerator to see what you need to buy. Also check to see if you should buy cleaning products.

When you know all the things that you need to buy, put them in a list. You may want to put the items in groups on your list. This will make it easier for you to remember to buy each item.

You can save money on the things you buy with **coupons.** A coupon is part of an ad that lets you buy an item at a lower price. If you have coupons for things you need to buy, put them with your list. Finally, check your list again to make sure you need all the items on it. You don't want to spend money on things you don't need.

2 SMART SHOPPING

Now that you have made your list you are ready to go shopping for groceries. As you shop, there are some things you should remember. These are put in two lists below: DOS and DON'TS.

DO

- Check the newspaper ads and the store ads for coupons.
- Try to stick to your shopping lists. Even $1 spent on extra items each item you shop is a lot of money over a year.
- Ask the store manager, the butcher and the people who work in the store for help or information.
- Read the labels on packages. They tell you important things about how much food is in the package and how good it is for you.
- Keep a total of how much money you have spent as you shop. It is easy to spend more than you planned on if you are not careful.
- Watch out for **specials.** A special is a lower price. You can save money if you buy items on special.

DON'T

- Shop when you are hungry. Everything looks good to eat and you may buy things you don't really need.
- Buy items you don't need just because they are cheap.
- Buy a lot of **perishable food.** Perishable food will spoil if it is not kept cold. If you buy too much, it could spoil before you can use it all.

OBJECTIVE

3   BUYING GOOD FOOD

Saving money when you shop is a good thing. But you also need to think about buying foods which are healthful, or good for you. You should read the labels on food packages. These labels tell you important things about the food. For example, they show how much sugar, salt, fat, and calories are in the food. Avoid foods with a lot of salt or fat. Both salt and fat can cause heart trouble.

Often these labels tell you the amount of vitamins or minerals in the food. Vitamins and minerals are things that your body needs each day. Foods that are high in vitamins and minerals are usually good for you. Fresh fruits and vegetables are very good for you. Sometimes they are more expensive than frozen food, but they are worth the extra money.

OBJECTIVE

4   UNDERSTANDING THE GRADES OF MEAT

Meat is a main part of many people's meals. Because people eat meat so often, it is important to know about the different **grades,** or types, of meat. Meat comes in three different grades: prime, choice, and good. This means that if you want to buy two pounds of hamburger, you have to choose one of the three grades of meat. Here is what the different grades mean.

1.   **Prime**   highest grade. Prime shows streaks of fat. It is tender and can be cooked quickly.
2.   **Choice**   high grade. Choice is also tender, but has more fat than prime.
3.   **Good**   good grade. Leaner and less tender than prime or choice. It takes more time to cook.

OBJECTIVE
5 THE FOUR BASIC FOOD GROUPS

Food is divided up into four different groups. This is because different types of food contain different things. Carrots have Vitamin A in them which is important for your eyes. Meat has the protein that your body uses for energy. Milk has calcium which makes your bones strong. Grains used to make bread can keep you from getting some types of cancer. As you can tell, your body needs each of these different foods. That is why it is important to eat something from each of the four food groups every day. Below is a chart of the four food groups. The chart also shows how much of each group you should eat each day.

The Four Basic Food Groups

1.   **Vegetables and fruits group**   four or more servings per day.
2.   **Meat group**   two or more servings per day. The meat group includes eggs, fish, and dried beans.
3.   **Milk group**   two or more servings per day. The milk group includes cheese, ice cream, and yogurt.
4.   **Bread group**   four or more servings per day. The cereal group includes grains, noodles, and rice.

REVIEW OF KEY WORDS

DIRECTIONS: Fill in each blank in the paragraph with a term from the list that follows.

coupons   **grade**   **groceries**
perishable food   **specials**

Sonia's refrigerator was empty. She knew she had to go shopping for _________________ (1) . She got the newspaper and cut out _________________ (2) so that she could save money. She also saved money by buying items that were _________________ (3) . She didn't buy certain items that were _________________ (4) because she knew they would spoil before she would eat them. She was also careful to choose the best _________________ (5) of meat, even though it cost more.

Check your answers on page 55.

CHECK WHAT YOU KNOW

DIRECTIONS: Circle the letter of the best answer.

1. Reading the dos and don'ts of food shopping helps you to save
   a. time.
   b. your job.
   c. money.
   d. all of the above.

2. You should not shop for food when you are
   a. alone.
   b. hungry.
   c. angry.
   d. upset.

3. If you want to save money on food you can
    a. check for newspaper coupons.
    b. check for store coupons.
    c. ask the store workers for help and information.
    d. all of the above.

4. Labels on food packages tell you
    a. how much the food costs.
    b. which part of the store the food is in.
    c. which vitamins and minerals are in the food.
    d. what other foods to serve with it.

5. Which one of the foods below is not part of the bread group?
    a. oatmeal.
    b. rice.
    c. cheese.
    d. noodles.

DIRECTIONS: Fill in each blank with the correct words.

6. Ask for ________________ if they are not displayed.

7. Don't buy items only because you have a _________ for them.

8. To be a smart shopper, you should know the ________________ of meat.

9. Read the ________________ on all packaged food.

10. ________________ and minerals are needed by your body each day.

Check your answers on page 55.

Number of Right Answers

REVIEW OF KEY WORDS   _________

CHECK WHAT YOU KNOW   _________

If you got seven or more answers right on "Check What You Know," you are ready to go on to "Using What You Know." If you got fewer than seven answers right, review this lesson. Re-read the objective for the question you missed. Then try to answer the Double Check questions that follow.

DOUBLE CHECK

DIRECTIONS: Match the terms in **Column A** with its definition in **Column B.** Write the correct letter beside each number.

<table>
<tr><td colspan="2">COLUMN A</td><td>COLUMN B</td></tr>
<tr><td>____ 1.</td><td>Specials</td><td>a. ads that can save you money</td></tr>
<tr><td>____ 2.</td><td>Prime</td><td>b. sales, good buys</td></tr>
<tr><td>____ 3.</td><td>Coupons</td><td>c. food, household supplies</td></tr>
<tr><td>____ 4.</td><td>Perishable food</td><td>d. a grade of meat</td></tr>
<tr><td>____ 5.</td><td>Groceries</td><td>e. likely to spoil</td></tr>
</table>

Check your answers on page 55.

USING WHAT YOU KNOW

DIRECTIONS: A list of dos and don'ts follows. Put a check beside each thing you should do when you go grocery shopping.

☐   1. Use a shopping list.

☐   2. Always buy in large amounts.

☐   3. Travel as far as you can to get specials.

☐   4. Buy whatever meat has the lowest price per pound.

☐   5. Read the package labels carefully.

☐   6. Look for specials.

☐   7. Keep track of your spending as you shop.

☐   8. Try to buy healthful foods.

Check your answers on page 55.

LESSON
5

Buying A Used Car

WHAT YOU WILL LEARN

OBJECTIVE 1   When you need a car.

OBJECTIVE 2   Deciding where to buy a used car.

OBJECTIVE 3   Learning how to choose a used car.

OBJECTIVE 4   Closing the deal.

OBJECTIVE 5   Paying for a car.

PRE-CHECK

DIRECTIONS: Check your *purpose* for reading. Each statement that follows is about one objective of the lesson. Read the statement. Then, put a check under your reason for reading that objective.

		YES, BUT I WANT TO REVIEW	NO, I WILL READ TO LEARN
1.	Can you list three reasons to sell your old car and buy a new one?	_______	_______
2.	Can you list three places where you might look for a used car?	_______	_______
3.	Can you list four ways to choose a good car?	_______	_______
4.	Can you figure how much money to offer when you're buying a used car?	_______	_______
5.	Do you know how to arrange a loan to pay for a new car?	_______	_______

38

PREVIEW

DIRECTIONS: Before you read the whole lesson:

1.   Read the title of the lesson.
2.   Read the key words and their meanings.
3.   Read the titles of each objective in the lesson.
4.   Read the first sentence of each objective.

Now you have previewed the reading. See if you can check the right answer for the following sentence.

You should sell your old car and buy another one when

☐   a. it has been driven less than 100,000 miles.

☐   b. it's five years old.

☐   c. it's giving you trouble.

Did you check *c*? Then you are ready to begin the reading.

Key Words

1.   **Annual Percentage Rate (APR)**   the rate of interest charged on a loan for one year. Before you buy a car, check the APR.

2.   **asking price**   the price the seller wants for a car. Make sure that you can afford the asking price.

3.   **Blue Book**   the official used car buying book. It is published by the National Automobile Dealers Association. This book lists the price ranges for all cars in the United States.

4.   **inspection**   looking at a car carefully to check its condition.

5.   **test drive**   taking a car on a drive before you buy it. You want to see how the car handles when you drive it.

1 WHEN YOU NEED A CAR

You may be looking for a used car. Maybe you don't own a car. But if you already own a car, when should you sell it and buy another one? Experts say that it usually pays to repair and keep a car unless:

- It has been driven more than 100,000 miles
- It is giving you trouble
- The car has a bad compressor, worn-out transmission, or broken differential

2 WHERE TO BUY A USED CAR

You can buy a used car from:

- New car dealers
- Used car dealers
- Private owners

Here is what you can expect from each of these:

NEW CAR DEALERS

GOOD POINTS	BAD POINTS
• take trade-ins	• higher prices
• give finance help	• commission to sales-person, other costs added to the price
• give guarantees	
• better service shop	
• used cars in better shape	

USED CAR DEALERS

GOOD POINTS	BAD POINTS
• take trade-ins	• commissions to sales-person and other costs added to the price
• give finance help	
• give guarantees	
• low prices	• condition of car may be poor

PRIVATE OWNERS

GOOD POINTS

- no overhead costs to include in the price
- can offer a real bargain
- can tell about car repairs and accidents

BAD POINTS

- will not take trade-ins
- will not finance
- give no guarantees
- car may be in poor condition

OBJECTIVE

3 HOW TO CHOOSE A USED CAR

Make sure the car passes your **inspection.** Inspect, or look over, the car carefully.

INSPECT THE OUTSIDE

- Look at the paint.
- Look for rust on the underbody of the car.
- Look at the exhaust and muffler for signs of rust.
- Look for oil leaks.
- Check the suspension.
- Check the shock absorbers.
- Check the tires.

INSPECT THE INSIDE

- Open and close all doors and the trunk.
- Check the windows. Open and close the vents.
- Look at the seats and check for worn springs.
- Look for signs of hard use: worn steering wheel, badly worn upholstery and carpet.
- Check the odometer for mileage.
- Check every switch in the car.
- Start the engine and listen for noises.
- Turn the steering wheel while the engine is running.
- Press the brake pedal.

UNDER THE HOOD

- Look at the engine.
- Check the cooling system.
- Check that the wires, fan belt, and hoses are not cracked.
- Check the oil.
- Check the transmission fluid.

TAKE THE CAR FOR A TEST DRIVE

- See if the parking brake works.
- Check both forward and reverse gears.
- Check the clutch if the car has a standard transmission.
- Drive 25 to 55 miles per hour to check high gear.
- Test the brakes.
- Check for vibrations in steering.
- Let the engine idle.
- See how the car handles on a hill.
- Turn on the heater, the air conditioner, the radio, and the windshield wipers.
- After the drive, check the exhaust.

OBJECTIVE

4 HOW TO CLOSE THE DEAL

Inspect the car and take it for a test drive. Then you can decide if it's the car you want to buy. You should find out how much the car is worth. The seller will give you a price, called *the asking price*. You will have to decide how much you are willing to pay for the car.

Get an idea of the price you should pay for the car. Go to your library and ask for **The Official Used Car Buying Book** put out by the National Automobile Dealers Association. This is also known as the **Blue Book.** It lists the price ranges for all cars found in the United States. You can check on the fairness of the seller's price in the Blue Book.

At the library, look at a copy of *The Consumer's Guide Used Car Ratings and Price* book. Also ask the librarian for the yearly automobile issue of *Consumer Reports* for the year the car was made.

Look in the newspaper for automobile ads. Find listings of cars for the same year. Look for the model you want to buy. Compare prices to get an idea of the value of the car. Think about whether the car needs any repairs, and then ask a mechanic how much it will cost to fix. Subtract this amount from the value of the car. This is the price you will offer to the seller. Sometimes you will be able to bargain on the price.

OBJECTIVE

5 HOW TO PAY FOR YOUR CAR

You may buy a used car from a private owner. You might have to pay cash. If your car is bought from a new or used car dealer, you will be able to pay for it over time. This means that you pay part of the total price of the car in cash right away. This is called the down payment. You pay the rest of the price little by little. Usually, you pay the same amount every month for two or three years. Because the dealer gives you more time to pay, there is interest added on to the price of the car. When paying for your car, here are some things you should know.

- If the down payment on the car is low, you will be paying money each month for a long time. This is because you are charged higher interest.
- Finance terms arranged by the car dealer are costly.
- The best interest rates on car loans will come from credit unions.
- Banks offer auto loans to people that have good credit ratings.
- Loan firms charge higher interest rates. But they will lend money to people who do not have credit.
- No matter where you apply for a loan, always ask for the **Annual Percentage Rate** (APR) you will be charged. If you know this yearly rate of interest, you can figure out the best deal.

REVIEW OF KEY WORDS

DIRECTIONS: Fill in each blank in the paragraph with a term from the list that follows.

Blue Book   **Annual Percentage Rate**   **test drive**
inspection   **asking price**

Charlie wanted to buy a used car. He wanted to know if the seller's _________________ (1) was fair. He took the car on the road for a _______________ (2). His _______________ (3) of the outside and inside of the car showed it to be in good condition. He looked in the _______________ (4) to check what the car was worth. When he applied for a loan, he asked about the _______________________________ (5).

Check your answers on page 56.

CHECK WHAT YOU KNOW

DIRECTIONS: Circle the letter of the best answer.

1. When your car's transmission can't be fixed, it means
   a. you have to walk.
   b. you should get another car.
   c. you have to use public transportation.
   d. you have to take the car to a new mechanic.

2. The seller who has no overhead is
   a. a new car dealer.
   b. a used car dealer.
   c. a private owner.
   d. a good friend.

3. You should inspect the car yourself because
    a. you are the best driver.
    b. you are the best mechanic.
    c. you want to see the shape of the car.
    d. you are going to have to paint the car.

4. Before you agree to pay a certain price for a car, you should ask a mechanic
    a. if he likes the car.
    b. to drive the car.
    c. if the car is a good model.
    d. how much it will cost to fix the car.

5. The best interest rates on car loans come from
    a. car dealers.
    b. credit unions.
    c. banks.
    d. loan firms.

DIRECTIONS: Fill in each blank with the correct words.

6. You should get another car if your car is giving your trouble and has been driven more than ____________.

7. A ________________ is the seller of a used car who can offer you a real bargain.

8. Look at the exhaust and muffler for signs of ________________.

9. The seller's price is called the ________________.

10. Financing the car ________________ to the total price you agreed on with the seller.

Check your answers on page 56.

Number of Right Answers

REVIEW OF KEY WORDS   ___________

CHECK WHAT YOU KNOW   ___________

If you got seven or more correct answers on "Check What You Know," you are ready to go on to "Using What You Know." If you got fewer than seven answers right, review this lesson. Re-read the objective for each question you missed. Then try to answer the "Double Check" questions that follow.

DOUBLE CHECK

DIRECTIONS: Match the term in **Column A** with its definition in **Column B.** Write the correct letter beside each number.

COLUMN A	COLUMN B
____ 1. New car dealer	a. reason to sell a car
____ 2. Bad compressor	b. check the tires
____ 3. Inspect the car	c. lend money to people who don't have credit
____ 4. Loan firms	d. the seller's price
____ 5. Asking price	e. where to buy a car

Check your answers on page 56.

USING WHAT YOU KNOW

Abbreviations in ads for used cars tell you about the features of the cars being offered for sale. Here are some of the abbbreviations you will come across in these ads:

air, a/c air conditioning

auto automatic transmission

bkt bucket seats

cpe coupe

cyl cylinders

int interior

mpg miles per gallon

p.b. power brakes

p.s. power steering

p. seat power seats

p. window power windows

Put a check next to each statement that describes a feature of the car in the ad below:

LeBARON '80

Auto, p.s., p.b., air, Am-Fm Stereo, p. windows, cruise control, luxury cloth interior, $5195.

☐ 1. The car has air conditioning.

☐ 2. The type of transmission is shown.

☐ 3. The car has power seats.

☐ 4. The LeBaron comes with power steering.

☐ 5. Power brakes are included.

Check your answers on page 56.

Post-Test

DIRECTIONS: Circle the letter of the best answer.

1. When you decide about housing, you should think about
   a. how much you can spend.
   b. where you want to live.
   c. how much space you need.
   d. all of the above.

2. Housing costs are often highest
   a. in cities.
   b. in the suburbs.
   c. in the country.
   d. on farms.

3. When you take a mortgage, the lender earns money from
   a. your down payment.
   b. the bank.
   c. the interest.
   d. the loan firm.

4. A written contract for rental is a
   a. loan.
   b. lease.
   c. down payment.
   d. mortgage.

5. Ads in the paper
   a. lists only expensive apartments.
   b. can help you find a place to live.
   c. are hard to find.
   d. are not helpful.

6. The abbreviation *per mo* means
   a. personal ads.
   b. rooms.
   c. per month.
   d. rent.

7. After you sign the lease
   a. nothing will be wrong with your housing.
   b. you cannot change your housing.
   c. you deal with the broker.
   d. you deal with the owner.

8. A tenant is
   a. an owner.
   b. a renter.
   c. a broker.
   d. a banker.

9. Smart shoppers don't
   a. plan with care.
   b. get the most for their money.
   c. read labels.
   d. waste their money.

10. You should compare
    a. brands.
    b. cost.
    c. value
    d. all of the above.

11. The unit price is
    a. the price per ounce, quart, pound, or count.
    b. the design of the package.
    c. the cost of the product.
    d. how long the product will last.

12. A house brand is
    a. something you make at home.
    b. something you find at home.
    c. the store's own product.
    d. a costly brand.

13. When you shop you want to
    a. spend all your money.
    b. follow your budget.
    c. only buy specials.
    d. only buy in large stores.

14. Eggs belong in the
    a. meat group.
    b. milk group.
    c. bread group.
    d. vegetable group.

15. Reading the dates on food products lets you know
    a. the price of the product.
    b. the size of the product.
    c. when you should stop using the product.
    d. the value of the product.

16. *Special* means
    a. low.
    b. far.
    c. small.
    d. on sale.

17. Keep your car unless
    a. it gives you trouble.
    b. you tire of the model.
    c. it's been driven less than 100,000 miles.
    d. your friend is a car dealer.

18. New car dealers
    a. refuse trade-ins.
    b. take trade-ins.
    c. charge the lowest price.
    d. always give the best deal.

19. You take the biggest risk when you buy a car from a
    a. bank.
    b. private owner.
    c. new car dealer.
    d. used-car sales person.

20. You take a car for a *test drive*
    a. after you buy it.
    b. within 6 months of purchase.
    c. before you buy it.
    d. for fun.

Check your answers on page 57.

ANSWERS

Pre-test

	ANSWER	LESSON	OBJECTIVE	SKILL
1.	b	1	1	Main Idea
2.	c	1	3	Detail
3.	b	1	3	Inference
4.	d	1	2	Vocabulary
5.	d	2	1	Main Idea
6.	a	2	3	Detail
7.	b	2	4	Inference
8.	a	2	1	Vocabulary
9.	a	3	1	Main Idea
10.	b	3	3	Detail
11.	a	3	5	Inference
12.	c	3	3	Vocabulary
13.	d	4	1	Main Idea
14.	b	4	4	Detail
15.	a	4	4	Inference
16.	a	4	2	Vocabulary
17.	d	5	1	Main Idea
18.	a	5	2	Detail
19.	c	5	2	Inference
20.	b	5	4	Vocabulary

LESSON 1   How to Decide About Housing

PREVIEW

Check *c*

REVIEW OF KEY WORDS

1. lease
2. rental deposit
3. equity
4. down payment
5. mortgage

CHECK WHAT YOU KNOW

	OBJECTIVE	SKILL
1. a	1	Main Idea
2. b	2	Detail
3. d	3	Inference
4. c	4	Detail
5. a	5	Detail
6. life	1	Detail
7. $2\frac{1}{2}$	2	Detail
8. real estate	3	Detail
9. more	4	Detail
10. needs	5	Detail

DOUBLE CHECK

1. b	2
2. d	3
3. a	3
4. c	5
5. e	4

USING WHAT YOU KNOW

1. Own
2. Own
3. Rent
4. Rent
5. Rent
6. Own
7. Own
8. Own
9. Own
10. Own

COMPETENCY

1.4.5   Identify information about the rights of a renter and the rights of a landlord.

1.4.1   Identify different kinds of housing.

LESSON 2   Finding a Place to Live

PREVIEW

Check *c*

REVIEW OF KEY WORDS

1. realtor
2. efficiency apartment
3. studio apartment
4. landlord
5. tenant

CHECK WHAT YOU KNOW

	OBJECTIVE	SKILL
1. c	1	Main Idea
2. b	2	Detail
3. a	3	Detail
4. a	4	Inference
5. a	5	Detail
6. available	1	Detail
7. duplex	2	Detail
8. evenings and weekends	3	Detail
9. fee	4	Detail
10. manage	5	Detail

DOUBLE CHECK

1. e	4
2. a	1
3. d	3
4. b	2
5. a	5

USING WHAT YOU KNOW

a, c, d, e, f

COMPETENCY

1.4.1   Identify different kinds of housing.

1.4.2   Interpret classified ads and other information to locate housing.

1.4.3   Interpret lease and rental agreements.

LESSON 3   How You Can Become a Better Shopper

PREVIEW

Check *a*

REVIEW OF KEY WORDS

1. unit price
2. house brand
3. generic product
4. net weight
5. RDA

CHECK WHAT YOU KNOW

	OBJECTIVE	SKILL
1. b	1	Main Idea
2. b	2	Detail
3. a	3	Inference
4. c	4	Inference
5. d	5	Detail
6. food shopping	1	Detail
7. comparison	2	Detail
8. unit	3	Detail
9. quality	4	Detail
10. labeled	5	Detail

DOUBLE CHECK

1. c	1
2. d	2
3. b	4
4. a	3
5. e	5

USING WHAT YOU KNOW

4

COMPETENCY

3.5.1 Interpret nutritional and related information listed on food labels.

1.2.2 Compare price or quality to determine the best buy for goods and services.

1.2.4 Compute unit pricing.

LESSON 4   Food Shopping

PREVIEW

Check *b*

REVIEW OF KEY WORDS

1. groceries
2. coupons
3. specials
4. perishable foods
5. grade

CHECK WHAT YOU KNOW

		OBJECTIVE	SKILL
1.	d	1	Main Idea
2.	b	2	Detail
3.	d	3	Detail
4.	c	4	Detail
5.	c	5	Inference
6.	specials	1	Detail
7.	coupon	2	Detail
8.	grades	3	Detail
9.	labels	4	Detail
10.	vitamins	3	Detail

DOUBLE CHECK

1.	b	1
2.	d	4
3.	a	2
4.	e	5
5.	c	3

USING WHAT YOU KNOW

1, 5, 6, 7, 8

COMPETENCY

3.5.2   Select a balanced diet using the basic food groups.

3.5.3   Interpret food storage information.

1.2.2   Compare price and quality to determine best buys for goods and services.

1.2.3   Compute discounts.

1.2.4   Compute unit pricing.

LESSON 5   Buying a Used Car

PREVIEW

Check *c*

REVIEW OF KEY WORDS

1. asking price
2. test drive
3. inspection
4. Blue Book
5. Annual Percentage Rate

CHECK WHAT YOU KNOW

	OBJECTIVE	SKILL
1. b	1	Main Idea
2. c	2	Detail
3. c	3	Inference
4. d	4	Detail
5. b	5	Detail
6. 100,000	1	Detail
7. private owner	2	Detail
8. rust	3	Detail
9. asking price	4	Detail
10. adds	5	Detail

DOUBLE CHECK

	OBJECTIVE	
1. e	2	
2. a	1	
3. b	3	
4. c	5	
5. d	4	

USING WHAT YOU KNOW

1, 4, 5

COMPETENCY

1.9.5   Interpret information related to the selection and purchase of a car.

ANSWERS

Post-test

	ANSWER	LESSON	OBJECTIVE	SKILL
1.	d	1	1	Main Idea
2.	a	1	2	Detail
3.	c	1	2	Inference
4.	b	1	3	Vocabulary
5.	b	2	1	Main Idea
6.	c	2	3	Detail
7.	d	2	5	Inference
8.	b	2	5	Vocabulary
9.	d	3	1	Main Idea
10.	d	3	2	Detail
11.	a	3	3	Vocabulary
12.	c	3	4	Vocabulary
13.	b	4	1	Main Idea
14.	a	4	4	Detail
15.	c	4	5	Inference
16.	d	4	1	Vocabulary
17.	a	5	1	Main Idea
18.	b	5	2	Detail
19.	b	5	2	Inference
20.	c	5	3	Vocabulary